sleeping

last straw strategies

last straw strategies
99 tips to bring you back from the end of your rope

sleeping

Michelle Kennedy

Creative Director PETER BRIDGEWATER
Publisher SOPHIE COLLINS
Editorial Director STEVE LUCK
Design Manager TONY SEDDON
Project Editor MANDY GREENFIELD
Designer JANE LANAWAY
Illustrator EMMA BROWNJOHN

Printed in China by
Hong Kong Graphics & Printing Ltd.
9 8 7 6 5 4 3 2 1

contents

sleeping
introduction

My favorite sport used to be biking. Now, it's sleeping. I honestly believe that the reason babies kick so much during the last three months of pregnancy is to prepare you for nights of continually interrupted sleep.

At a baby shower I listened quietly as a group of new moms described with much anguish their perpetual lack of sleep. Things seemed to be particularly difficult for moms who were breast-feeding or stayed at home, because they felt the onus was on them to care for the baby at night. Suddenly one of the women turned to me and asked, "So, how do you do it?"

Caught. Now, I'd have to admit to being the world's laziest mother. Eventually, I figured out a way to sleep and keep my baby happy. Instead of sitting in a rocking chair and nursing, I started bringing baby into bed with me. I nursed him while lying on one side and then placed a towel on my chest, burped him, and rolled over with him to nurse on the other side. "You can do that?" one of the mothers said. "You bet," I replied. "It works great during the day on the couch, too!" Just make sure that you don't fall asleep nursing your baby.

Here are nine sections-worth of other helpful bedtime hints to take you from newborns to preschoolers.

through the night?
yeah, right

It is a common misconception that with the right schedule any baby will learn to sleep through the night. Unfortunately, that is far from the case. In the beginning, most babies will wake up throughout the day (and hence, the night) almost every hour or two. My advice for new parents? Get used to it. It's going to happen. Hopefully, if you work, you will be able to get those first two months off so that you can adjust. If not, make sure dad is helping. If you're nursing—heck, even if you're not— bring baby to bed with you and eliminate the need to keep getting up and going to him.

give up the schedule!

through the night? 0–6 months

"When will my baby start sleeping through the night?" the new mom of a two-week-old asked me. Controlling the temptation to say, "You're kidding, right?" I simply replied that all babies are different. True enough, but if you give up expecting that your one-month-old will sleep straight through, then you'll be less upset when you wake up at 2 A.M. Oh, by the way, it's a well-known fact that small babies only sleep for several hours at a stretch during the day—never at night!

through the night?
rapid response . . .

I always go to the kids when they cry. The one time you don't go may be the one time something is really wrong—a fever; pain from a tooth; baby caught in the crib. I'm just not willing to take that chance. Sometimes I creep in quietly on my hands and knees to see what the problem is without their noticing!

through the night?
. . . or not
6 months–2 years

Another mom says, "I have made the mistake of going into my daughter's room at every whimper, and it really caused problems . . ." This is a common scenario. It's hard, especially at first, to hear a baby (after the newborn stage) start to whimper and restrain yourself from going to her. But it is a necessary evil, if you wish her to start getting back to sleep on her own. Try and ignore the little whimpers, assuming of course that you know her to be all right (dry, fed, and so on). Help her get back to sleep on her own by leaving her be. "Now," this mom said, "to get her to bed initially, we try and have her play quietly."

through the night?

baby boot camp

If your baby wakes up late in the morning to help make up for some of his late nights, begin waking him at an earlier time each day to help encourage him to get the sleep he needs at night—when the rest of the household sleeps.

through the night?

power naps

0–2 years

Check your baby's napping habits (*see Naps, pages 34–47*).
A journal can really help in this area. Just like old people,
babies who spend too much time visiting the People's
Republic of Nod during the day sometimes have difficulty
sleeping at night. Keeping a journal, and asking other care
providers to do the same, will help clue you in to when and
how long your baby is taking naps. Many times a baby-sitter
could be allowing your child to sleep for three hours or
more close to what is normally your bedtime—causing all
kinds of problems for your schedule! If he is taking naps that
are way too long, either readjust his schedule or put him in
a well lit area for his daytime snoozes, so that he'll only
sleep when he feels really tired, without oversleeping.

through the night?

no distractions

Babies who wake up in the night may have been distracted from feeding properly during the day. Some babies don't seem very interested in daytime feeds—they are often too caught up in what is going on around them to suck properly. Try to carry out your daytime feeding in a quiet, darkened room, so that she can concentrate on the job at hand and get a complete feed.

through the night?
finish what you start 0–12 months

When nursing, make sure that your baby empties the first breast completely. After he has nursed on the same breast for a period of, say, 10–20 minutes (depending on the rate at which your baby sucks), he gets the rich, high-calorie milk known as hindmilk, which he needs for energy and growth. This milk will fill him up a bit faster and satisfy his hunger, whereas the first milk from the breast (the foremilk) satisfies only his thirst. Getting the hindmilk may also help to space out his nighttime feeds—one of the reasons formula-fed babies often sleep longer at night is because it takes their tummies longer to digest the richer formula, and the same is true of hindmilk.

the real thing

Is your baby using a pacifier? He may enjoy sucking it so much that he is not paying enough attention to nursing from you. Try offering the breast instead of the pacifier during the day. Regular daytime nursing sessions may help to reduce his middle-of-the-night waking.

If it's the dependence on a pacifier you don't like (in my case, the hospital nursery started my first-born on one before I knew any better to say anything about it), offer baby your knuckle to suck on. I often used my breast as pacifier, but sometimes I just wanted to put the closed sign up, and a clean knuckle worked just as well.

rock-a-bye

0–12 months

When it gets toward evening, strap your baby in a carrier or a baby sling and get on with what you usually do (not cooking, though!). Your movement and closeness will help to keep your baby relaxed, encouraging doziness and an easy transition to sleep.

to bathe or
not to bathe?

Most babies (and indeed most adults) feel sleepy after a soothing, warm bath. However, if splashing about in water stimulates your little one, switch bath time to mornings or another time of the day.

through the night?
nighttime is
for sleeping

0–12 months

Let your baby know this in as many ways as possible. For instance, nurse in a darkened room at night if he wants to feed. Change diapers right there in his crib or in your bed, in the already dark and relaxed room, rather than flipping on the light and waking up both you and him—keep a closet or bathroom light on for illumination. Take him into bed with you to nurse. This will let you snuggle down and rest your eyes while he is getting a much-needed snack, and he will respond to your relaxed mood. Once your baby has finished feeding, you may want to put him back in his crib to sleep, for safety's sake.

the family bed
time to share

Share a room. If the idea of letting baby sleep with you is unappealing, then at least bring him into your room so that you don't have far to reach—or stumble—to get to him in the middle of the night. Cute nurseries are great, but in the beginning, keep it practical. You're also a lot more likely to get some help from dad if the baby is screaming in a bassinet at the foot of the bed! And doctors advise that babies should sleep in their parents' room for the first six months, to reduce the risk of crib death, or Sudden Infant Death Syndrome (SIDS).

soothing touch

0–12 months

If your baby does wake in the night, this is a proven way to get him back to sleep without picking him up. Sit next to him while he lies in his crib, stroking/rubbing/singing/talking him to sleep. My friend did this, and while her son cried, she would reassure him and stay by his side, but she did not pick him up. She said it took less and less time to send him off, and now her son can fall asleep all alone.

the family bed

the sidecar

This is a great solution for people suffering from sleep deprivation. How can something that brings such great sleep to everyone in the family be bad? A good majority of us grow into adults who end up sleeping with their partners, so I think it can be a good thing for children to get used to having a warm body next to them at sleep time. We have a family bed set up in a sidecar arrangement, using a three-sided crib connected to the bed. The baby usually goes to bed around 8 P.M., after bath, story, and cuddles. If she wakes up, we go to her and help her settle down. She nurses throughout the night, but for the most part doesn't wake up.

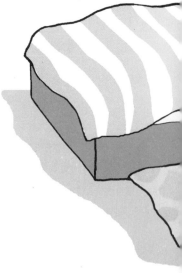

the family bed
temporary camp 1–4 years

Does your child like his room for only some of the night? Do you find yourself with a cuddly visitor at three in the morning, who soon becomes a tossing and turning circus act? I love the feeling of a snuggly four-year-old seeking comfort between my husband and me, but soon my bundle of joy has his feet over my neck and his head buried in my husband's side. There comes a point when your baby is just too big to sleep with. So set him up next to you on the floor—just keep a sleeping bag and pillow next to your bed. And if he wakes up and needs to be near you, he has his own, yet separate, space.

the family bed

everyone on the floor

0-4 years

One of the best decisions I ever made was to put us all on the floor in one bedroom: me, my husband, and our first two children, who are 14 months apart. I put two futon

mattresses (a double and a single) next to each other on the
floor of my bedroom and there was plenty of room for all
of us to lie down. I could nurse, change diapers (of both the
newborn and the 14-month-old), and ease a nightmare—
all from the comfort of one bed. And yes, eventually all my

children slept on their own (all four
of them now thoroughly enjoy their
own beds). But for those early days,
when sleep was at a premium,
having everything in one room
was a life- (and sleep-) saver.

the family bed

halfway house

Would you really rather that your child stays in his own bed? Compromise. Tell him that he can come in and snuggle with you when the sun comes out—in the summer, this will be pretty early, but he might fall back asleep for a while.

On the bright side, if you have to get up anyway, a snuggling cutie pie in your bed is much more pleasant than a beeping alarm clock!

the family bed
exclusion zone
2-4 years

If your child is becoming more at home in your bed than her own, and you don't like it, make sure that you keep your bed—and maybe even your bedroom—off limits. Don't let the children play in your room or watch TV on your bed, even during the day. Don't let your bed be an option for them. Do all of the fun, loving routines in her bed instead. Read books there, rub her back, talk and sing with her, tell her stories, cuddle her. Make her feel that her bed is the "place to be," and then you can reclaim your own without fear of it being taken over by your little one.

the family bed

sleeping positions

If you are breast-feeding, sleep facing your baby. This
will enhance your sleeping awareness of his presence,
and will make breast-feeding more convenient when your
still-asleep baby starts to get hungry and restless during the
night. It is best not to put him next to dad, because sleeping
fathers tend to be less aware of their babies than sleeping
nursing mothers are. If you are not breast-feeding, then
place your baby between you and a protective guardrail,
such as you would install on a toddler's bed. Be sure that
his face is not covered by either a blanket or comforter and
that he is not lying on a pillow.

make it cozy

0–2 years

Warm up baby's bed. Sometimes it's not the other bodies baby wants, but just the warmth in the bed. Cool sheets shock grown-ups, too, so one mom said that she warms her son's crib sheet with a hair dryer before she lays him down—preventing a wake-up before he is even in bed.

the family bed
rice bag comforter
0–6 months

Make a rice bag out of the leg of an old pair of pants, and
1 pound (500g) of rice. Simply cut off one pant leg about
24–28 inches (38–46 cm) long. Stitch closed one end of the
cut-off pant leg, and pour in the rice. Stitch the other end
of the cut-off pant leg closed. To use, place the rice bag
inside the microwave and heat on high for two minutes.
Or, you can wrap it in tin foil, and place it in a regular oven

for 15–20 minutes at 350°F (175°C). (Remove foil wrap before using.) Give the rice bag a good shake, and make sure it isn't too warm. Then get a T-shirt (or any type of shirt) you have worn, but not yet washed. Wrap it around the rice bag. The rice bag will hold its heat for about 30–40 minutes. Before nursing or rocking baby, place the rice bag in the crib or bed. It will warm up the bed nicely, so that when you remove the rice bag and lay baby down, he won't be disturbed by a shift in temperature. And that smelly T-shirt? The warmth of the rice bag fills baby's crib with the wonderful scent of you. If you use a family bed, the warm rice bag is great to tuck next to baby, as you creep away. The scent-filled bag will make baby think you are still near by.

the family bed

bed coverings

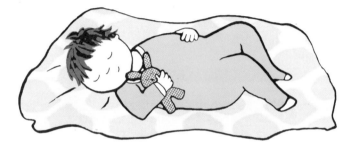

Use a firm mattress or a hard (as in old, compressed) futon, preferably placed on the floor. Mattresses, if still in their frames, should fit tightly. A sidecar arrangement is ideal since it allows mom to be right next to baby, but they maintain separate sleeping spaces. Avoid using thick comforters or fluffy pillows, which pose a risk of suffocation. For colder nights, just dress baby in a warm, footed sleeper and omit any bed coverings. I hated the idea of getting rid of my pillow altogether, so I folded it in half to keep it out of her way.

the family bed

making more babies   0-12 months

So, what's a couple with a healthy, active sex life to do?
Your house has other rooms, right? You might think that
by establishing a family bed, the nights of spontaneous
lovemaking are over. This does not have to be the case. You
simply have to choose either a different location or time,
other than your own bed or bedtime, for sex. Or, if you are
sharing your bed with only one child, you might remove him
to his own bed after he falls asleep. It may take some time,
but you and your significant other will find a tactic that
works. Other family-bed parents suggest that the necessity
to find other locations for intimacy adds spontaneity to
lovemaking. This is just one more positive aspect of the
family bed: it not only leads to a closer relationship with
children, but can also create a special bond between parents.

naps

sleepy time

I don't know who needed the naps more when my kids were small, them or me. But whomever they were for, sometimes it sure is difficult getting them to take one. I never made a huge deal out of schedules for naps, only because I knew that if we had had a quiet morning without a lot of physical activity, then a nap would probably not be necessary. However, if we spent the morning at the park or running errands, I knew they would sleep for a while. As with everything else, be flexible. An enforced quiet time is always good, even if a nap isn't happening.

make it special

6 months–4 years

It can be hard to put a child down, especially when older children, who don't take naps, are home. So, make this a special time for you and the napper. Tell the older kids to go play in their room or outside, then cuddle with the sleepy guy. Read together or play a short game of Memory, then snuggle him in. It's a great way to get the younger child to slow down after a morning of riding high with those energetic older brothers or sisters.

baby won't sleep
out of your arms?

Transfer your baby from your arms to his bassinet with a song that you begin singing while he is lying on you. Continue to sing this song as you lay him in his own bed. Your continuous singing will occupy his auditory sensory channel, leaving him mesmerized. He may stir, but the sound of your voice, as you place a hand on his back for one minute, will probably calm him. Then gently remove your hand, but keep singing softly to him. He may indeed stir again and even begin to cry. If he cries, place your hand on his back again—do not pick him up—and repeat the whole process. Continue to sing to him for a few moments after he has calmed down.

reset baby's internal clock

0–12 months

If your baby is waking up with the lark or going to sleep very early, then try and get her hours back into alignment. Hang a comforter over the window if it's getting bright very early, or try and extend her day artificially by bringing bright lights into her world at night. Do it gradually; she's still going to be sleepy at 6 P.M. the first few nights, so try and increase her activity level by 15- or 30-minute increments. Eventually, her days and nights should even out a bit to match yours.

naps
everybody do it
0-4 years

Make nap time a universal quiet time. This is particularly
important if you live in a small house (like I do) and have
a lot of noisy people around (like I do!). If the weather is
bad and there is a lot going on inside, make sure
that nap time for one is quiet time

for everyone else, too. This is a great opportunity for all the kids to take a break for an hour and read, draw, or even play a game quietly. It also gives me a sanctioned reason for not being able to do any noisy chores—and I get a chance to do some reading, too!

naps

hot water bottle 0-12 months

One mom suggests putting baby to bed with a hot water
bottle. Make sure that the water is tepid, not boiling, and
then cover the bottle with a throw or pillowcase that you
yourself use. Place baby on her back, the position that
doctors recommend to reduce the risk of Sudden Infant
Death Syndrome (SIDS) occurring. Then put the hot water
bottle at the bottom of the crib (or remove it)—it (or
the residual heat) will keep baby nice and warm while
she naps, with the comforting smell of mom nearby
at the same time.

naps
fresh air

0-2 years

Maybe it's stuffy inside, or maybe it's the coolness of the breeze, but some babies just sleep better outside. Take baby for a walk, go to an outdoor café or the park. Bring a book along. Or, open the window in the room where the baby is napping. If you are worried about the direct breeze or safety issues, open the top part of the window, or get a small, oscillating fan and point it above the baby's crib. It will circulate the air without blowing directly on your little one.

extreme nappers   0–12 months

Does your baby sleep for four or five hours at a time during the day and then wake up constantly during the night? You're not alone. One mom solved this problem by putting the baby's crib in the living room during nap times. The baby

would fall asleep among the noise and activity when he was really tired, but when he was waking up, instead of falling back to sleep, he heard the activity and wanted to join in. His naps were shorter and he slept better at night.

naps

nap wars

1–4 years

If nap time becomes a battle or a full-blown power struggle, step back. You can't make your child go to sleep—and if you try, you will lose. Tell her she does not have to go to sleep, but she does have to have a quiet time during which she rests her body. Let her choose where she will rest—her bed, a darkened family room, the recliner, and so on. She can also choose which stuffed animal or "quiet toy" she can have with her. If you give her a few choices, the struggle will resolve itself sooner.

avoid catnaps

Catnaps are generally troublemakers. A 5–10 minute snooze can upset a child's rhythm for the rest of the day and even into the night. Be especially wary of car rides, swings, or feedings—all of which are good catnap inducers. This doesn't mean, of course, that if your child falls asleep on the way to the store you should wake him up, but if you notice a trend (again, that journal can be handy!) of catnaps and a lack of real naps, then perhaps you need to restructure his nap schedule or your activities.

naps
household humming 0–12 months

When your baby is napping, don't tiptoe around the house feeling afraid to flush a toilet, shut a door, or squeak a floorboard; you want him to be able to sleep through all the different noises of normal household activity.

naps

0–12 months

the right place

Be careful not to let your baby nap exclusively in the baby carrier, a stroller, or a car seat. At least some of the time he has to nap in his crib or bed. If he becomes too accustomed to certain places, he might not be able to nap anywhere else. There is a part of me that says, "Let him sleep at the kitchen table, if it makes him fall asleep!" And for the most part, that's true. But this is a useful tip for anyone who might be on the go with baby a lot; if your child is always falling asleep while moving, then the crib is going to pale in comparison. Again, restructuring activities to allow for a quiet nap time (at least most of the time) should alleviate dependence on carriers, strollers, and car trips. But hey—if baby is screaming and will only fall asleep this time on a car ride—then don't let me stop you: get driving!

from crib to bed
transitions

If your son can get out of the crib, it's time for the crib to go! That's a long fall from the top rail of the crib, and he could get hurt. Children are ready for a bed at different times, and it's not hard to tell—most kids will let you know. The day will come when your child will get excited about a big boy's bed and want one of his own. He thinks that the crib is only holding him back, but at night he really does like that security. So, make the transition a safe and easy one, ensuring that the bedding you use is suitable, if it is not standard issue. And don't force it—he will not (I repeat, will not) ask you to set up his crib in his college dorm room. Won't happen, I promise.

first steps

2-4 years

Why not try a toddler bed? This is a small bed that snugly fits a crib-sized mattress and has a guardrail on the side. It's inexpensive, and the crib mattress will allow your child to keep his familiar bedding while he's in the new setting.

from crib to bed

why move?

One mom says that if your child likes her crib and isn't climbing out, there's no need to move her into a bed. My son was content in his crib until about a month ago—he never did climb out, just complained a lot about going to bed. I finally got him a twin bed with special "Space Jam" sheets. We are using a railing from a bunk bed to keep him from falling out. He has only climbed out of it once and is very happy with his big bed. But I waited until he told me he was ready for a big bed! In my opinion, you need to follow your child's lead. When she's ready to make the move, she'll let you know (either by climbing out or complaining).

from crib to bed
ground rules

2-4 years

In the beginning, put a mattress on the floor and let your child play on it for a week or so. Then ask if she would like to sleep on it for naps. Keep the crib in the room if she is still attached to it. Eventually, try taking the crib out of the room. You know what they say: "Out of sight, out of mind."

from crib to bed

big boy's bed

When my son was three, we wanted him to start sleeping in his big boy's bed. So we'd wait until he fell asleep with us, then moved him to his room. By waking up in his own bedroom, he got used to sleeping by himself, and after a month he was able to fall asleep in his new bed. This may not work for all children, but it's worth a try.

from crib to bed
night wanderers 2-4 years

Are your children getting out of bed a lot? Are you concerned that they will be roaming around the house and possibly getting hurt? One dad suggests putting a gate in front of their door, which you can use at night, so that they can't wander around the house. Seem like jail? Maybe, but so is a crib. And being safe is always more important. Besides, who among us does not have the house practically cordoned off in a variety of childproofing mazes? This way, at least, your children can play, you can feel reasonably secure in knowing they can't go anywhere and hurt themselves, and with a bit of luck, they'll fall back asleep after a little midnight romp.

from crib to bed
2-4 years **farewell ceremony**

If you've kept the crib in your child's room, let him sleep
there at night, but encourage him to use his new bed during
playtime or for naps. Over time, he'll adjust to the idea of
spending the night in it. When he's finally ready to make the

switch, mark the crib's removal with a good-bye kiss or some other small ceremony. Above all, remember that even if those first few nights are a bit bumpy, every child eventually adjusts—usually without major upheavals.

from crib to bed

the daybed

Is your toddler ready to leave the crib, but still not ready for a regular bed? Try giving him a daybed instead. A daybed has "rails" on three sides and these, coupled with a guard rail on the open side, will give your child the comfort and security of a crib, while at the same time offering him the room and freedom of a regular bed. The daybed can either become your child's permanent bed, or you can use it temporarily and then promote it to use as a guest bed later on, when your toddler has finished with it and has moved on to a regular bed.

old friends

Give your child a familiar toy to take to bed and cover him with his old blanket—even if it's too small. Keep his bed on the same side of the room and in the same position that his crib was in. If you're worried that he might fall out, put a bar up by his bed and a cushion on the floor. Also, don't take his bottle or pacifier away while he's getting used to his bed; that may be too much at once.

from crib to bed

2-4 years

party time

Throw a "big-kid bed" party. Choose a date and talk up the event a week in advance. On the big day, create a party atmosphere and invite some friends and the grandparents along to witness the arrival of the new bed.

soft options

2-4 years

Let him pick out his own soft coverings for his new bed. One mom said she gave her child two types of bedding to choose from, plus a matching border to go around his room.

"He thought it was great that he picked out his own stuff. We also set his bed up several months beforehand so that he could check it out and become completely comfortable with it. He thought he was so grown-up when he moved to that bed! But I think some people try to rush it. If you don't need the crib, what is the big deal if they aren't ready for the regular bed?"

from crib to bed

big brother

When we moved to our new home, my husband and I found ourselves in the downstairs bedroom and our four children shared the upstairs bedrooms.

Our four-year-old, who often used to come into our room early in the morning, began climbing into the bed of his ten-year-old brother, who kindly put up with him. Maybe our older son snores, but after a few days, the four-year-old began sleeping right through the night in his own bed. I have a feeling he just got used to waking up in his own territory and decided that it was more comfortable to sleep in his

 own space, surrounded by his own things. And other moms have found that having their kids share a room can help get rid of bad sleeping habits and temporary sleeping problems.

I'm not sleepy
toddlers

My beautiful daughter had fallen asleep in the car on the way home from a late night at a friend's house. I carefully carried her all the way from the car seat to her bed, undisturbed. She was very tired. As I gently laid her upon her bed, she bolted upright, looking shocked that I was putting her into bed. In my most Mary Poppins of voices I said, "Lie back down, darling, and go to sleep." And in her most throaty and loud voice she yelled, at the top of her lungs, "I'm . . . not . . . sleepy!" And then she proceeded to fall asleep. They think they know best, but guess what? We know better.

beat the clock

2-4 years

Set an egg timer for 15 or 20 minutes and watch them scramble. Make a deal that pajamas have to be on, teeth must be brushed, and everyone must be sitting on their beds awaiting tucking in (and a story) before the buzzer goes off. Everyone who beats the clock gets another story (or another sanctioned extra). Once they have learned to beat the timer, you could occasionally surprise them on a Friday night by letting them stay up late as a treat.

I'm not sleepy
2-4 years **talking time**

One mom says that she and her partner struggled for
quite some time with getting their children to stay in bed.
"My husband and I eventually found ourselves dreading
bedtimes. We have always done the usual rituals before
they get into bed, but they never seemed to help them relax
enough to actually stay in bed and go to sleep. (They are
five and six now.) We finally found something that works
to help them relax: we call it "talking time." We give the kids
an extra 10 or 15 minutes to tell us three things they were
proud of, or that they liked, during their day. It helps reduce
separation anxiety, helps them to relax, and really boosts
their self-esteem. Plus, I really enjoy spending time with
them, listening to their thoughts and feelings."

catching a yawn

1-4 years

Yawning is a subconscious signal to others that we are tired and want to go to sleep.

It is also infectious.

So, sit by the crib or on the bed, so you can be seen, and start yawning.

If anybody else comes in, get them to yawn as well.

Your wide awake child will not be able to help copying you and, with luck, will doze off (as you probably will, too).

Apparently, the yawn is an evolutionary part of our body language. In prehistoric times, when we lived and hunted together in groups, a good, undisturbed night's sleep was essential to a successful hunt the next day. The infectious yawn was a signal that it was sleeping time for everybody.

I'm not sleepy
1-4 years
toy bedtime

A great way to make a sleepy but cranky toddler understand
that it is time for bed is to have her take you by the hand
and lead you around her room, putting all the toys to bed in
their closets or boxes. You can give them each a little pat, or
cover them up with a blanket, and tuck them in. Talk a little

about why the toys "need" their sleep (lots of busy
roboting to do tomorrow). It's a great way to straighten
up a cluttered room, too.

I'm not sleepy

1-4 years   # quiet time

After dinner, send kids for an early bath, then have a family treat, such as a story or movie. The key is to make everyone relax, and not just the kids. When even older kids and parents participate, it helps little ones calm down. Once in a while, I try to surprise the kids. Sometimes, we will sit out on the deck in the dark and look through a telescope, or light outside candles or torches and play shadow puppets on the wall of the house. In the winter, you can surprise kids by popping up some popcorn while they are in the bath (thinking that their evening is over) and letting them stay up late to watch a gentle TV show or play a board game.

I'm not sleepy
when I was a child . . .   1-4 years

Children love it when their parents tell them stories from their own childhood or school experiences. It is also a good way to pass on family history and values. My children beg to hear stories about when I was a child. I highly recommend it as an occasional alternative to reading books.

I'm not sleepy

give them a fair warning

1-4 years

This is especially helpful if your kids are engrossed in something in particular. Instead of saying, "Time for bed," give them 20-, 10-, and 5-minute warnings. This way they make sure they finish whatever they are doing. It also leaves no room for excuses!

I'm not sleepy

tuck him in tenderly
1-4 years
and then be tough

Take your time while you tuck in your toddler and make sure that he is really comfortable. But once the hugs and kisses are done, help him to understand it is time to go to sleep. Be firm and responsive to any questions, but don't encourage him to ask more. Whenever possible, answer his questions from the doorway so your toddler doesn't succeed in luring you back into the room. This is hard because you want to be a good parent and explain why the sky is blue, but sometimes you have to end it. Simply tell your child that Mommy is sleepy too and wants to go to bed, so can we go to the library and get a book about that tomorrow? If that doesn't work, then a sweet, but firm, "Hush now, I'm going to bed," coupled with another kiss will suffice; then walk away. I promise, you're not being mean.

I'm not sleepy
1-4 years
progress chart

Elizabeth Pantley, author of *Perfect Parenting*, suggests creating a "Bedtime Chart." Use a large piece of poster board on which you number and illustrate each step of the routine. For example, "put on PJs," "have snack," "brush teeth," "read some books," "potty," "turn on night-light," "kisses and hugs." You can check off each item with a marker. You can also expand the chart to include morning routines.

I'm not sleepy

bedroom, not prison

1-4 years

Avoid using your toddler's room or bed as a sin bin. Sending your toddler to her bedroom when she has misbehaved may work well for discipline purposes, but it may also cause problems when you want her to go to bed at night. She will have trouble thinking of her bedroom as a pleasant place to be and may become more reluctant to go to sleep there. If possible, designate another room or a specific area in your home as the exile corner. She'll then associate that spot, rather than her bedroom, as the place of correction when she's been naughty.

I'm not sleepy
a mad half-hour

Sometimes it helps to let your child get any pent-up energy out of her system before you try to settle her down for the night. My youngest son runs around like a crazy person for 15 minutes or so each night before going to bed. He chases the cats, wrestles his brothers and sister, or just jumps up

and down. On cool evenings, even the older ones will take a few laps around the house to get rid of some of that excess energy. Just be sure to follow up with a soothing bath and a story to get them back in a calm frame of mind.

monsters under the bed
night frights

In the dark, everything changes. Coat racks become vampires. Bedposts become monsters. Lumps of unfolded laundry become wild dogs—or worse. For active kids with active imaginations, the dark can be a quiet, scary place. It seems silly to us grown-ups sometimes, but your child's imagination is wondrous: the same imaginative mind that sees horses in the clouds during the day also hears the bogeyman under the bed at night. A reassuring tone and a couple of these tips should help to shoo the monsters from your child's room.

monsters under the bed
tell monster stories

1-4 years

One mom helped her kids defeat the bedtime monsters by
making up monster stories with them. By giving the children
a "monster dictionary," she gave them a vocabulary to use
to identify, and thus defeat, their fear. Think of names,
habitats, and hobbies for the monsters. And make sure none
of them lists "small children" as
their favorite food—better to
list pizza, or peanut butter and
jelly, just like your little one!

monsters under the bed
glow-in-the-dark

Almost everything glows in
the dark these days: posters,
stars, and planets to stick on
the walls; stuffed animals. Take
your child to the toy store
and find some fun items
that glow in the dark to
keep her company until she

falls asleep. Together with a night-light, these should help
your little one feel safe in her own room. The chance to gaze
up at her stick-on stars will give her a reason to look forward
to the dark, rather than to fear it.

monsters under the bed
watch what they do 1-4 years

That scary monster lurking in the corner could be the villain in a cartoon, particularly if you turned the TV off just before going to bed; or it might be the evil creature in a story you have just been reading together. My own son started thinking about the villain in a video game while he was settling down to sleep. Remember, just as we sometimes anguish over our own villains (bills, workloads, schedules, and the like) as we are trying to get off to sleep, so our children anguish over the things that bother them most, which then come to haunt them during the hours of darkness. So watch what they watch just before going to bed, and try and keep the monsters at bay.

1-4 years
monster spray

A friend of mine said that her goddaughter went through this phase when she was about four. Her mom made a "monster spray" to keep the nighttime monster away. It was water (because monsters don't like to get wet), garlic powder (because monsters don't like the smell), sugar (because monsters aren't sweet), and blue food coloring (the color of the daytime sky, because monsters only like the night) in a squirt bottle. Before bedtime every night it was sprayed at the door and windows and around the bed, and monsters were told to stay away because the room was protected with magic spray. The bottle actually only contained water with a little blue food coloring, but my friend's goddaughter didn't know that! Inform a few other special people, such as grandparents or close family friends, about the magic spray. This way, it will only take a quick bedtime phone call to reinforce its effectiveness. The spray worked well. And after a short period of time, it wasn't even needed anymore.

monsters under the bed

good monsters

Don't let her forget that some monsters are good guys. Cookie Monster, Elmo, Grover—all from *Sesame Street*—are nice monsters. They would definitely intervene on your little one's behalf, if she asked them nicely. You can write a quick pretend postcard to Elmo, or another friendly monster, asking him to talk with any mean monsters. He's certain to oblige. You can surround your child with images of good monsters, too. If you have a stuffed monster, he can be placed on guard to "talk" to any bad monsters that might come your way. Draw pictures with your child of what her idea of a "good" monster should look like. Let her know that if she only pictures the good ones, surely they will be the only ones to come and visit.

monsters under the bed
magic dust

1-4 years

This works on the same principle as monster spray. Shake
a little talcum powder or cornstarch mixed with a bit of
glitter around the perimeter of the room. It's just like
drawing a line in the sand—the monsters can't cross it.

monsters under the bed

make a sign

Get out the best poster board, markers, paints, or crayons you have, and sit down with your child and design an elaborate "no monsters allowed" sign. While you're making the sign, try to talk about the reasons why your child is so afraid. Maybe even ask her to describe what the monsters look like. Talking through her fears may help to eliminate them.

monsters under the bed
mom rules

One mother said that her son was afraid of monsters at nighttime, so one night she said, "Okay, monsters in Michael's room, it's time to go home. Your mommies are looking for you." Her son got a real kick out of this and it seemed to work. Much of this type of success is simply because you are letting your child know that you believe him. If you simply dismiss a child's claim of monsters with a, "There's no such thing as monsters," you are telling him that you think he's either lying or not worth protecting. By standing up for your child, you are acknowledging what he sees and giving him the confidence that you will stand by him—whether facing monsters or whatever.

king of the world

Make him the brave protector of his own domain. I told my son, Alex, that he was the king of Alexworld, and that he didn't have to let anyone into his kingdom whom he didn't like (although this got a bit sticky with his older sister!). He was also the designated protector of his world, which included his stuffed animals, his action figures, and the like. It was his job to tell the monsters to retreat, and because he was the king, they had to do exactly what he said.

Just remind him now and again that when he wakes up in the morning, he's back in Mommyland— and Mommy is without doubt the supreme ruler of Mommyland!

monsters under the bed
throw them out

As your child directs you to where those nasty monsters hide, go around the room and make sure they leave. Pretend to be angry that there could be monsters lurking in your child's room—and make sure the monsters (and your child) know that they are not welcome back.

security guards

1-4 years

Does your child have a particular stuffed animal that looks like it could handle a scary monster? Put it on guard in front of the child's door. It sounds silly, I know, but if you instill in the stuffed animal the power of "Mommy," your child will feel safe. Most children know that a stuffed animal is only a stuffed animal, and won't need him to stand guard for very long; just the fact that you wanted your child to be guarded is often enough to make monsters go away. And it's definitely better than having to sit there yourself all night!

early risers
dawn raiders

Nothing like a peaceful Saturday morning. No rushing around. No work to do. Just sleeping in and drinking coffee. Ah, keep dreaming because for your little one, Saturday is just another day and, if it's morning, it's time to be awake. My youngest loved to come into my room first thing in the morning (like 5 A.M.) and announce, "I awake now!" Translated: "Let the games begin!"
If you are like me and would desperately like to get a couple more minutes, heck, even hours, out of your sleep, then don't give up—there is sleep out there—you just have to do a little planning and a lot of hoping in order to go out and bring it home.

early risers
keep it dark
0-12 months

Don't turn on bright lights during nighttime feedings and changings. Use night-lights, holiday lights, tap lights (little round lights that you tap to turn on), a red bulb in a special lamp—anything to keep the light dim and to keep baby in a sleepy frame of mind.

up with the sun

Is your toddler awake with the sun (which means pretty early in the summer months)? Set her up with some

puzzles, games, or favorite toys at her bedside when she goes to sleep. Encourage her to play for a while in the morning before waking up everyone else.

cut down on naps

1-4 years

Does your toddler take two naps during the day? Move her to one at midday. One nap? Then start a during-the-day quiet time instead of a sleep, when your child sits on the couch and reads, or plays quietly on the floor—even watches TV if it helps. Of course, if a nap is essential, then let her sleep, but you could probably wake her in a half hour or so, rather than letting her nap longer. Otherwise, you could try cutting out some of the naps on certain days —for instance, my own preschooler started taking just a two-hour nap every other day.

early risers
1-4 years **pushing back bedtime**

Ease bedtime later and later. This won't work if it's not gradual and consistent. Putting a three-year-old to bed at 10 P.M. when he's used to going to bed at 8 P.M. will only make for a crankier kid at 6 A.M. So ease bedtime back 20 minutes at a time: three days at 8:20 P.M.; three at 8:40 P.M.; and eventually your child will be ready for a 9 P.M. bedtime—and hopefully a 7 A.M. wake-up!

head up

Stuffy baby? Does baby have a bad cold? You can help him to sleep and keep him from waking up at night by propping up his mattress slightly. Just take a blanket or pillow and put it under the crib mattress, propping up baby's head a bit and helping him breathe easier. Don't prop up baby with a pillow or blanket inside the crib because that's a suffocation risk. Alternatively, you can prop up the whole crib by placing phone books under two of the legs. If you're nursing and baby is sleeping with you, instead of laying him flat on the bed to nurse, prop him up in the crook of your arm and let him sleep that way, too (although you will probably have to change sides to keep your arm from falling asleep!).

early risers

1-4 years

hunger pangs during the night

Maybe he's hungry? Many kids go to bed not long after dinner and wake up—or are cranky first thing—because they're hungry. Try easing back bedtime a bit, but also giving a snack before bed. It doesn't have to be dessert. It can be yogurt, carrots—even a peanut butter sandwich! This might help tide your little one over until a more palatable hour. Another solution—if your toddler is allowed to roam the house upon waking—is to keep something that he can eat before breakfast ready for him in the morning. Put a granola bar or a mix of dry Cheerios and raisins in a baggie and leave it on the kitchen table.

your own little alarm clock

1–4 years

One mom sets an alarm clock for her little one. Decide on a time, like 7 or 7:30 A.M., and when the alarm goes off, then the little one can come out to play.

early risers

1-4 years

here comes the sun

Check out your child's room early one morning. It could be that he's waking early because the sun comes in and shines right on him in bed. Consider rearranging the furniture or installing room-darkening shades to keep the room dark in the morning. Even tilting upward the slats of blinds that you already have might deflect much of the harsh morning sun.

early risers
wet and dry
1-2 years

Does your child wake up early because of a very wet diaper?
If so, cut down on drinks before bedtime, particularly milk
and cranberry juice, which tend to make people need to
pee more! On the other hand, if your little one is getting up
because he is thirsty, start keeping a water bottle next to his
bed. The kind with the straws coming out of the top works
great. You can also hang it from your child's headboard with
a cup holder like those sold for cars. (They hang from the
car window.) Just be sure to fill it only with water because
sugary juices can ruin teeth (by sitting in the mouth all
night); they also make your little one even thirstier because
sugar is dehydrating.

early risers

self-service breakfast

Would you like a couple of extra minutes to yourself in the morning? You would be surprised at how resourceful preschoolers can be. I actually came out of the shower one morning to observe my two-and-a-half-year-old (I was silent and watching from behind the wall) pouring his own glass of chocolate milk. He didn't spill a drop and I was shocked! But to avoid the inevitable disaster with a full gallon of chocolate milk, I started putting a glass of juice on a low shelf in the fridge for him the night before. We also put out bowls of dry cereal along with a plastic cup of milk (just the right amount) so that he could pour it on his cereal himself. He is so proud of himself for "making his own breakfast," and I get to blow-dry my hair while it's still wet!

wait a bit 6 months–2 years

If you are certain that your baby or toddler is just awake, and not in any sort of pain or danger, wait a few minutes before going in to him—because once you're there, he's going to wake up all the way. If you wait 10 or 15 minutes, he might find a way to snuggle back in for a rest.

nightmares
sleep tight

There is nothing worse than waking up while it is still dark outside with the vague image of an awful nightmare in your head. Nightmares, just like dreams, are very real—certainly to the people who live through them. Everything you see, everything you do in the nightmare feels like you really did it. And your body can be just as tired as if you really had done all of those things. Bear this in mind when comforting a little one who has just woken up with a nightmare. Saying, "It was just a dream," is often of little comfort to someone who just spent an hour or more running from the school bully . . .

bright lights

We found that our little guy was scared of the dark so
we strung Christmas lights in his room to keep it dimly lit.
After that, he stopped screaming when he woke up at night.

nightmares
1-4 years

keep calm

Plan quiet evening activities. Don't read scary picture
books or allow your child to watch scary movies or TV
before bedtime. Give your child a bath, wrap up with her in
a cozy blanket, and then either read or watch TV together.
Teach her a game of cards, or get down on the floor and
build something out of building blocks with her. I like to get
on the floor and lay on my tummy with the kids while we
watch TV. It makes me feel a bit like I did when I was a kid
(except when I have to get back up), and the kids seem to
like me being on their "level."

light in the dark

nightmares

1-4 years

Leave a light on and keep the bedroom door open if she wants you to do so. Now is not the time to talk about being a "big kid" since embarrassing your child about her fear of the dark, or dismissing it without respect for her feelings, will only serve to deepen it.

nightmares

comfort

If your child wakes up crying, sympathize with his fears and remain with him until he calms down. It is important to stay in your child's room rather than invite him into yours. By letting your child regain his composure in his own room, you help him to see that his own space is safe after all.

soothing noises

nightmares

1–4 years

Is your child afraid of nighttime noises? Creaking stairs. Wind through the trees. A tree banging on the roof. Cars driving by. A dog barking. All these are normal sounds, but at night, when you're alone in your bed, they can seem awfully strange. Help your child combat the nighttime noises with a soothing sound of her own. Near her bed, place a tape player—with headphones if necessary—and keep a tape in it of music that your child likes. There are some great tape players for toddlers and preschoolers that are easy for little hands to use (and sturdy). Just make sure the tape has the sweet sounds of a lovable and soothing voice, and not the Stones' tape you were trying to get her to enjoy earlier in the day. That way, the last thing she hears before she drops off will be calming sounds that will lull her to sleep.

thunder and lightning

Thunder and lightning are not only scary when they
are going on, but they can make for a restless night once
they're over. Try and make a game of thunder and lightning.
Count between the flash and when the thunder comes—
one second for each mile the lightning is from you (not
steadfast, but a good rule of thumb). You also can make up
stories about what could be causing the thunder. (When
I was a kid, we said that the angels were bowling; a really
loud boom was a strike.) During the day, you can find
different materials, such as poster board or tin foil, and
rattle it so that it makes a thunder sound. Getting used
to the idea of the noise helps kids not to be afraid of it.
One night, the kids and I had a raucous time trying to
outdo a real thunderstorm with our pieces of cardboard.

talking it over

Avoid talking about the details of the nightmare when your child wakes up frightened. Talking about it will only serve to remind her of the scary points. In the morning, if she wants to, you can talk about the dream or draw a picture about it in the safety of daylight.

nightmares

2-4 years

going to the bathroom

Ask her if she would like to go to the bathroom. Sometimes the urge to go to the bathroom disturbs sleep, intruding on a peaceful dream and causing stress—much in the same way that an alarm clock ruins an otherwise peaceful morning snooze.

don't be a hero

nightmares

2-4 years

Do not make her feel that you have "saved her" or protected her from anything, or that she is safe only when you are present in the room. In other words, don't act the hero. Make your child feel that she is capable of handling the situation herself, by showing her (if she is scared of shadows or monsters, for example) that she was perfectly safe before you came into the room. If it's nightmares she's suffering from, then let her know that once she wakes up, she's safe— that just by waking up, she has saved herself from whatever was frightening her.

nightmares
     like clockwork

If your child wakes up every night at a regular time, set your alarm a half hour earlier and wake him up (gently and briefly) *before* he wakes up with a nightmare. Comfort him a bit, then let him get back to sleep. The idea is to break the regularity of the nightmare cycle.

catch the bad dream

nightmares

1–4 years

Develop some nighttime rituals, and if your child is constantly having bad dreams, try something a little different: a "dream catcher" is a popular Native American item that catches bad dreams and lets only the good ones through. You can either make one with your child or buy a ready-made one. All you need to make a dream catcher is a hoop (an embroidery hoop or bent wire hanger will work well), some yarn, and some colorful beads. Arrange the yarn around the hoop in a spiderweb fashion, hanging beads off here and there. Then hang the dream catcher in your child's room to capture those nightmares.

you and . . .
your partner

Even though your baby has made you a family of three,
the two of you still need time together as a couple to
keep that relationship strong. Because your lives are
busier now, the best way to find that time is to plan for it.
Try to make a regular weekly "date"—schedule a sitter
and head out to dinner or a movie. If you don't want to
leave your baby with a sitter just yet, make a special
dinner at home after you put the baby to bed.

you and...your partner
sleep together

If you and your partner want to spend any time together,
you have to be able to stay awake for adult time. The best
advice I ever got was to take a nap when my baby did.
Forget the pile of dirty dishes! You're tired—sleep! Dishes
and tax returns can be done when baby is awake, happily
next to you in a portable bassinet or baby carrier.

115

you and...your partner
outside help

Get into nature. Sunshine and green surroundings are good
for all of you. Going outside together, with your baby in a
bouncer, baby carrier, or stroller, can be a great stress reliever.

stay up late

Staying up after the baby is sleeping also can give you time to connect daily. Strive for at least 20 minutes a day to talk and share your feelings with your partner; you can do this while you wash the dishes together or even as you get ready for bed. The most important thing is to use your creativity to find a way to spend time together that works for you, whether that means meeting for lunch while a willing grandparent watches the baby, getting a friend to baby-sit while you both go for a jog in the park together, or playing a game of cards before you go to bed.

you and...your partner
go courting

Go out on a date. Arrange
for evening baby-sitting.
If cost is an issue—
or if you'd just feel
more comfortable
leaving the baby
with someone you
know—look into

starting a baby-sitting co-op, a group of parents who rotate
evenings out and sit for each other. And remember, you
don't have to have a full-fledged night on the town: the goal
is simply to get out for some time alone with each other.
So take a walk, grab a bite, go to the movies.

stay in

Make a date night at home. You don't need a sitter to pay attention to each other. Once your baby has settled down for the night—or at least for a few hours—grab some couple time. Resist collapsing on the couch and switching on the TV, or slouching off to finish work. Sit together for some face-to-face time with a glass of wine or a cup of herbal tea. Focusing on each other for as little as 10 minutes can make a huge difference. All too often, new parents can forget even to make eye contact with each other. By simply carving out some inviolable moments together you'll feel more connected and in touch.

you and...your partner
get creative

Time for each other doesn't have to take place in the
evenings. For instance, you can use your commute time
to be together. Grab lunch together. It's surprising how

animated
conversation can
become when
you're meeting in
the middle of the
day and there is
no baby or batch
of chores to
worry about.

book ahead

Buy season tickets or book in advance. If you've already paid for seats at a concert, theater, or sporting event, you'll feel committed to going. To cut the cost of such an evening, arrange to swap baby-sitting with another couple. This is a great idea and one I wish I could have gotten started in my neighborhood; it seems like it would work great in an area with a community center, or if you already have friends with kids. Start a cooperative for baby-sitting: every couple or parent announces when they can baby-sit and takes on another couple's children. Each hour you sit, plus each kid, is a "credit" toward an hour of baby-sitting for you. You can spend the credits when you like, depending on the rules you have devised for your co-op. It's a great way to make friends and get out (knowing that your children are in the hands of a trusted individual) at the same time.

you and... your partner
take a break

Treat weekends like weekends. Pack the diaper bag, take out the stroller or a backpack, and enjoy a weekend activity as a family. Museums, malls, parks, outdoor events, and the like are all baby-compatible these days, so there's no excuse for not making the effort.

you and...your partner
your own agenda

Plan regular treats, like a weekly video and take-out dinner night. Once your baby settles into a predictable bedtime, life really changes (yet another great reason to work toward instituting a regular bedtime). Renting a video is a cheap and easy way to enjoy a little downtime together. If all you have is two or three minutes together before family life intrudes, then hug, kiss, give each other a quick neck massage . . . Take a deep breath and go back to your life. You'll connect, even if it's only briefly, and everything else will get done.

you and...your partner
create some
post-work rituals

Try taking a walk together every evening with your baby.
Your little one gets some fresh air, and you two really can
connect at the day's end and catch up on each other's news.

you and...your partner
play games

Games are great distractions—and a great way to have fun together, so dust off the chess set, a deck of cards, Monopoly board, or whatever else promises to help you forget the sleeping volcano next door. I think there comes a time in every relationship when you feel—especially with children—that all of the life has been sucked out of your brain and you really can't think of anything interesting and un-child-related to say to one another. It may sound a bit corny, but beating my husband at backgammon (we're not talking about my losing gin rummy streak) always perks up my competitive edge and gives us something to do that doesn't require too much brain power! Also, games are easily set down when a child starts to wail.

further reading

KARP, HARVEY, MD.
*The Happiest Baby on the Block:
The New Way to Calm Crying and
Help Your Baby Sleep Longer.*
New York: Bantam Doubleday Dell
Publishers, 2002.

MINDELL, JODI A.
*Sleeping Through the Night: How
Infants, Toddlers, and Their Parents
Can Get a Good Night's Sleep.*
New York: HarperCollins, 1997.

PANTLEY, ELIZABETH, AND
SEARS, WILLIAM, MD.
Perfect Parenting.
New York: McGraw-Hill/
Contemporary Books, 1998.

PANTLEY, ELIZABETH.
*The No-Cry Sleep Solution: Gentle
Ways to Help Your Baby Sleep
Through the Night.*
New York: McGraw-Hill/Contemporary
Books, 2002.

SEARS, WILLIAM, MD, AND WHITE, MARY.
*Nighttime Parenting: How to Get
Your Baby and Child to Sleep.*
New York: Plume, 1999.

WEISSBLUTH, MARC.
Health Sleep Habits, Happy Child
New York: Fawcett Books, 1999.

notes

Acknowledgments

I would like to thank my children, my husband,
Rebecca Saraceno, and Mandy Greenfield.

index